# Herding Dogs

By Mary Ann Hoffman

Gareth Stevens
Publishing

Please visit our Web site, www.garethstevens.com. For a free color catalog of all our high-quality books, call toll free 1-800-542-2595 or fax 1-877-542-2596.

**Library of Congress Cataloging-in-Publication Data**

Hoffman, Mary Ann, 1947-
Herding dogs / Mary Ann Hoffman.
    p. cm. — (Working dogs)
Includes index.
ISBN 978-1-4339-4656-1 (pbk.)
ISBN 978-1-4339-4657-8 (6-pack)
ISBN 978-1-4339-4655-4 (library binding)
1. Herding dogs—Juvenile literature. I. Title.
SF428.6.H64 2011
636.737—dc22

2010035243

First Edition

Published in 2011 by
**Gareth Stevens Publishing**
111 East 14th Street, Suite 349
New York, NY 10003

Copyright © 2011 Gareth Stevens Publishing

Designer: Michael J. Flynn
Editor: Kristen Rajczak

Photo credits: Cover, pp. 1, 5, 9, 14, 17, 20 Shutterstock.com; pp. 6, 10, 13, 18 iStockphoto.com.

Printed in the United States of America

CPSIA compliance information: Batch #CW11GS: For further information contact Gareth Stevens, New York, New York at 1-800-542-2595.

# Contents

Words in the glossary appear in **bold** type the first time they are used in the text.

Herding dogs move other animals. Many different dog **breeds** can be trained as herding dogs. Herding dogs work with cattle, goats, sheep, reindeer, and other animals. Some work well with any kind of animal. Some work with only one kind. We'll look at two types of herding dogs: heelers and headers. They move herds in different ways. Heelers work from the back of a herd. Headers work from the front.

# Dog Tales

Dogs have helped herd sheep since the 1570s!

Herding dogs are sometimes used on farms to gather ducks, chickens, turkeys, and geese, and move them as a group.

# Dog Tales

Heelers are very active. As pets, they need a home where they'll get a lot of exercise and attention.

Some herding dogs may be small, but can move animals three times their size.

# Heelers

Heelers are herding dogs that direct and move animals by jumping and nipping at the animals' heels. Heelers are very smart and watchful dogs. They have a lot of **stamina**. They are very quick and like to run. Heelers usually work at the back of a herd. They are trained to control the movement of the herd and keep the animals moving forward. Heelers can make very good family pets.

# Headers

Herding dogs that keep a herd together and work to turn the animals and even stop them are called headers. Headers continually move around a herd. They move to the front of the herd when they want the animals to move in a certain direction or just stay together in one place. Headers are very **focused** when doing their job. They gather animals together and keep them within areas.

## Dog Tales

Some herders use "eye" to move animals in a herd or get them to stay where they are. They give the animals a very direct stare.

This border collie is telling a group of animals what to do.

## Dog Tales

Breeds that make good herding dogs have extra-thick coats to keep them warm and dry when they're working outside.

Herding dogs work closely with their **handlers** during training.

# Training

Breeds that make good herding dogs are smart, strong, and can work for long periods of time. They stay interested and active in what they are doing. Herding dogs are trained to obey voice commands, hand movements, and **whistles** made by their handlers. The dogs practice obeying commands, moving around a herd, and directing a herd. These exercises are very important parts of a herding dog's training. Most herding dogs start training when they are puppies.

# Working Hard

The dog breeds used as herding dogs are naturally good at gathering, moving, and keeping animals together. However, training them to do these activities by following set commands takes a lot of time and effort. During training, the same commands and actions are done over and over. Every mistake a dog makes is corrected so the dog learns exactly what to do. Herding dogs are trained to stay focused on their task.

This border collie has learned to keep the sheep together. Herding dogs know how to bring back animals that leave the group.

# Dog Tales

The blue heeler is born with a white coat. It changes to blue in about 2 weeks. Blue heelers also have tan or black markings.

Australian cattle dogs usually weigh about 40 pounds (18 kg) and can be 17 to 20 inches (43 to 51 cm) tall.

# Australian Cattle Dogs

Different breeds can be trained as herding dogs. Let's look at some of the most popular ones.

The **Australian** cattle dog is sometimes called a blue or red heeler. Blue and red heelers are quick, watchful, **obedient**, and smart. They're strong. They can be very independent, so good training and handling are important. This breed is a natural herder. The dogs jump and nip at the legs of cattle. They'll nip at the heels of people, too, to get them to move in a certain direction.

# Welsh Corgis

The Welsh corgi is a small herding dog. Corgis are only about a foot (30 cm) high at the shoulder. Being low to the ground keeps them from being kicked when they're moving and directing a herd. They're quick and run in half circles. They nip at the heels of the animals they're herding. Corgis are smart, strong, and active. They herd both cattle and sheep.

# Dog Tales

There are two types of corgis—Cardigan and Pembroke. The Cardigan is used more for herding. Pembrokes are kept as pets.

A Welsh corgi's large ears help it hear well.

# Dog Tales

Border collies herded sheep in the hills of England and Scotland during the 1800s.

The border collie lowers its body and creeps along the ground as it works. It raises its head and uses "eye" to get animals to obey!

▷

# Border Collies

Border collies are herding dogs that work at the front of a herd to keep it together. They're trained to **respond** very quickly to the commands of their handler. Border collies are excellent runners. They're also known for being able to stop and switch directions in a flash! Border collies are very strong, medium-sized dogs. Most have black-and-white fur. Border collies are fast, calm, and have a lot of energy.

# Old English Sheepdogs

Old English sheepdogs are herding dogs that are easy to recognize. They have beautiful long, thick coats that are grey and white. They're strong, obedient, and smart. Though large, Old English sheepdogs move quickly and can cover a lot of space in a short amount of time. They like to have set areas to work in. Old English sheepdogs use their size to herd animals. They even bump into the animals!

## Dog Tales

An Old English sheepdog has hair covering its face and eyes. The hair helps protect its eyes!

# Herding Dog Commands

| Herding Command | Meaning |
| --- | --- |
| come-bye | move in a clockwise direction |
| away to me | move in the opposite direction of clockwise |
| stand, lie down | stop or slow down |
| look back | look for lost animals |
| hold | keep the animals together |
| walk up, walk on | move calmly toward the herd |
| get back, get out | move away from the herd |
| that'll do | return to the handler |

# Glossary

**Australian:** from the country of Australia

**breed:** a group of animals that share features different from other groups of the kind

**focus:** to keep attention and effort on

**handler:** a person who trains and controls an animal

**obedient:** follows directions

**respond:** to act after something has happened

**stamina:** the ability to keep doing something without getting tired

**whistle:** a high-pitched sound

## Books:

Miller, Marie-Therese. *Hunting and Herding Dogs.* New York, NY: Chelsea Clubhouse, 2007.

World Book, Inc. *German Shepherds and Other Herding Dogs.* Chicago, IL: World Book, 2010.

## Web Sites:

### Dog Owner's Guide: Herding Trials
*www.canismajor.com/dog/herdtrl.html*
Read about border collies and how they are trained and tested.

### How to Love Your Dog: A Kid's Guide to Dog Care
*www.loveyourdog.com*
Learn training techniques for your dog.

# Index